Turkey travel guide 2024

Majestic Landmarks: An Exploration into Turkey's Ancient Wonders

Beatty s Kelley

TABLE OF CONTENT

CHAPTER ONE

CHAPTER TWO

CHAPTER THREE

CHAPTER FOUR

CHAPTER FIVE

CHAPTER ONE: INTRODUCTIONS TO TURKEY

Welcome to the magical crossroads of Asia and Europe, where history unfolds like a colorful tapestry and cultural variety beckons at every step - this is the Turkey Travel Guide 2024. Nestled between two continents, Turkey serves as a time bridge, inviting visitors to discover its rich past, beautiful landscapes, and dynamic cities.

In this detailed book, you'll go on a trip that goes beyond the commonplace and immerses you in Turkey's fascinating tapestry. Turkey, with its thousands-year history, is a treasure mine of archeological treasures, historical towns, and architectural marvels. From the famed Hagia Sophia in Istanbul to the ancient ruins of Ephesus, every corner tells a narrative of civilizations that have left an everlasting stamp on this region.

Istanbul, the city that spans two continents, is an excellent starting point for exploring Turkey's cultural riches. Explore the bustling Grand Bazaar, where the sounds of merchants bargaining have echoed for centuries, and marvel at the stunning combination of East and West in the architecture of Hagia Sophia and the Blue Mosque.

Beyond the metropolitan attraction, Turkey's landscapes are as varied as its history. Cappadocia, with its strange fairy chimneys and cave houses, promises to transport you to a realm straight out of a fantasy novel. The blue seas of the Mediterranean and Aegean shores attract leisure and aquatic activities, resulting in a beautiful coastal retreat.
Turkey's food is a gastronomic joy, and our guide explores the culinary riches that define Turkish cuisine. From the exquisite kebabs and mezes to the sweet pleasure of Turkish delight, every mouthful is a celebration of tastes steeped in history.
Explore the cultural complexities that distinguish Turkey as a one-of-a-kind location as you read this guide. Experience the soothing rituals of ancient Turkish baths (Hamams) and the spiritual dance of the Whirling Dervishes, all of which represent the nation's rich legacy.
These book not only reveals historical and cultural beauties but also offers practical tips for navigating modern Turkey. Understand the complexities of transportation, from efficient public transit to scenic road excursions. Stay educated on safety precautions and healthcare amenities to ensure a smooth and pleasurable trip.

Turkey in 2024 invites you to a world where historical heritage blends with modern energy. If you're looking for historical echoes, different food delicacies, or the warmth of Turkish hospitality, this book will take you on a trip that transcends time and captures the spirit. Join us as we discover Turkey's timeless beauty and cultural diversity.

Overview of Turkey

Embark on a captivating odyssey through the allure of Turkey with the Turkey Travel Guide 2024. Nestled at the crossroads of Asia and Europe, this enchanting nation boasts a kaleidoscope of cultural influences, breathtaking landscapes, and a history that unfolds like an ancient manuscript.

The overview of this travel guide provides a panoramic glimpse into the diverse experiences awaiting the adventurous traveler. Istanbul, the vibrant metropolis straddling two continents, introduces visitors to the heart of Turkey's cultural richness. Iconic landmarks like the Hagia Sophia and the Blue Mosque beckon, while the bustling Grand Bazaar immerses visitors in centuries old market traditions.

Beyond the urban landscape, the guide explores the natural wonders that grace Turkey. Cappadocia, with its whimsical fairy chimneys and cave dwellings, unveils a surreal landscape reminiscent of a dream. The Mediterranean and Aegean coasts lure with their turquoise waters, offering sun-soaked escapes and a plethora of water activities.

Culinary enthusiasts will find delight in the exploration of Turkey's gastronomic treasures. From succulent kebabs to flavorful mezes and the sweet indulgence of Turkish delight, the cuisine is a celebration of diverse influences and regional specialties.

Practical considerations are seamlessly integrated into the overview, offering insights into transportation options and safety considerations. Whether navigating bustling city streets or serene rural landscapes, the guide ensures that travelers are well-equipped for a seamless and enriching journey through this captivating nation.

Turkey, in 2024, invites you to traverse its timeless landscapes, immerse yourself in its cultural treasures, and savor the flavors of its culinary delights. Let this overview be your key to unlocking the secrets of Turkey – a destination where ancient legacies meet modern marvels in a harmony that captivates the senses and captures the heart.

- ## Historical and cultural significance level

Turkey's travel tapestry is delicately woven with threads of historical grandeur and cultural richness, beckoning visitors to uncover the layers of importance that have defined this country. The Turkey Travel Guide 2024 brings history to life by combining historical marvels and cultural traditions to create an exciting trip through time.

Istanbul, the mesmerizing city, is a living witness to Turkey's historical significance. The Hagia Sophia, an architectural marvel that has seen empires rise and fall, and the Blue Mosque, with its elaborate tilework, symbolize the Byzantine and Ottoman legacies that have left their imprint on the cityscape. The Grand Bazaar, a maze of busy market streets, reflects the dynamic trade that has distinguished Istanbul for centuries.

Beyond the city limits, Turkey possesses ancient monuments that transport visitors to bygone eras.

Ephesus, an ancient city that once rivaled Rome, reveals its well-preserved remains, including the famous Library of Celsus and the Great Theatre. Troy's fabled tales of the Trojan War provide a magical dimension to Turkey's historical story. Turkey's cultural significance stems from its traditions and customs. The tour digs into experiences such as the Turkish bath (Hamam), where the cleaning routine transforms into a sensory adventure infused with centuries-old rituals. The captivating Whirling Dervishes, Sufi mystics, perform a mystical dance that transcends time, providing a look into the heart of Turkish culture. Turkey Travel Guide 2024 reveals a fascinating collection of sights and locations that entice visitors to experience the country's various landscapes and historical riches. Istanbul, a city that spans continents and vibrates with the energy of a bustling metropolis, is one of the crown jewels. The Hagia Sophia, a masterpiece of Byzantine architecture, and the Blue Mosque, covered with exquisite tiles, are also prominent sites. The Grand Bazaar, a labyrinthine bazaar, entices with centuries-old customs and colorful displays of merchandise. **Cappadocia**, located in Anatolia, reveals a surreal dreamscape with fairy chimneys and cave houses.

Hot air ballooning over this strange location provides a stunning view, making for an unforgettable experience.
The ancient city of Ephesus, located on the Aegean shore, is a fascinating archeological site. The Library of Celsus and the Great Theatre bring tourists back to the glory days of Rome, giving them a sense of antiquity's grandeur.
Pamukkale, often known as the "Cotton Castle," is a natural marvel in southwest Turkey. White travertine terraces with warm mineral-rich waters form a dreamlike environment. Hierapolis, an ancient spa city, lends a historical dimension to this geological marvel.
The landscapes around the Mediterranean and Aegean shores provide not only sun-soaked retreats but also historical sites. The remains of Troy, buried in mythology and old legends, provide a mythological dimension to Turkey's rich historical past.
As the book navigates these sights, it also discovers lesser-known treasures hidden away in Turkey's many provinces. From the historic city of Hattusa to the mysterious vistas of Mount Nemrut, each location adds to the charm of this enchanting country. Whether lured to the lively city life or

seeking comfort in the quiet of ancient ruins, the Turkey Travel Guide 2024 assures that each visitor encounters a unique tapestry of experiences. Throughout the tour, narratives emerge of a country where history resonates in every cobblestone and culture is woven into the fabric of daily life. In 2024, Turkey welcomes you to embark on a journey that will not only explore its historical magnificence but also celebrate the cultural tapestry that characterizes its present and future.

CHAPTER TWO

Getting started

Exploring Turkey's cultural mix and historical treasures in 2024 is an exciting idea, and the "Getting Started" section of the Turkey Travel Guide is your indispensable guide for a smooth journey. This section acts as a compass, helping you through the first stages to guarantee a smooth and rewarding discovery of this fascinating country.

First and foremost, understanding the visa criteria is critical. The book gives up-to-date information on required papers, ensuring you are well-prepared for your Turkish excursion. Whether you're planning a short vacation or a longer stay, obtaining the correct visa is the key to discovering Turkey's wonders. **Currency and practical travel** information are the next concerns. Turkey's official currency is the Turkish Lira (TRY), and learning about local traditions and etiquette will improve your vacation experience. The guide provides information on tipping procedures, market bargaining, and basic etiquette to assist you navigate daily life with cultural awareness.

Timing is critical, and the guide will help you choose the ideal dates to visit Turkey based on your tastes. Understanding the climate and peak seasons improves your vacation planning, whether you're drawn to the excitement of cultural festivals, the serenity of historical monuments, or the attraction of seasonal landscapes.

Transportation is another important consideration, and the book describes the numerous alternatives available. Understanding Turkey's diversified transportation environment allows you to explore at your leisure, from efficient public transit systems in large cities to scenic road excursions that lead to hidden jewels.

Safety concerns and healthcare information are also easily integrated into the "Getting Started" section, offering critical insights for stress-free travel. Whether you're traversing crowded city streets or tranquil rural surroundings, the guide will make sure you have the knowledge you need to make the most of your Turkish journey.

As you begin on your Turkish adventure in 2024, let the "Getting Started" section serve as your road map, taking you through the crucial planning components. With a strong understanding of visa procedures, local customs, optimal travel times, transit alternatives, and safety precautions, you are well-prepared to see Turkey's attractions.

Visa requirements and travel logistics

Visa Requirements: Your passport must be valid for at least six months beyond your departure date. Most nationalities require a visa to enter Turkey. Depending on your purpose of visit, you can apply for a tourist visa online or when you arrive. Check the most recent visa requirements and application procedures, and prepare the appropriate papers.
Tourist Visas: Most travelers to Turkey need a tourist visa.
Apply for an e-Visa online before your travel or get one when you arrive at Turkish airports.
Your passport should be valid for at least six months after your scheduled departure date.
E-Visa Application Process: Visit the Republic of Turkey's e-Visa webpage.Fill out the online

application form with precise personal and travel details.
Pay the visa cost securely using the online platform.
Visa-on-Arrival: If acquiring an e-visa in advance is not possible, you may usually receive one upon arrival at Turkish airports.
Make sure you have all of the relevant documents, such as a valid passport and evidence of lodging.
Business and work visas: If you intend to do business or work in Turkey, a visa may be necessary. For specific requirements, contact the Turkish embassy or consulate in your own country.
Student Visas: Students wishing to study in Turkey must apply for a student visa.
Acceptance letters from Turkish educational institutions, as well as confirmation of financial resources, are required.
Medical Tourism Visa: For persons seeking medical treatment, a medical tourist visa may be required.Include documents from the medical facility that detail the treatment plan.
Transit Visas:If you are traveling from Turkey to another country and want to exit the international transit region, you may need a transit visa.
Important considerations:

Carry a copy of your e-visa or visa-on-arrival paperwork with you at all times during your visit. Comply with visa restrictions to prevent penalties or issues during your trip.
Note: Visa requirements are subject to change, so check for the most recent updates and particular laws based on your nationality before planning your trip to Turkey in 2024.

Places in turkey where currency exchange is located

Turkey's official currency is the Turkish Lira (TRY). Inform your bank of your travel dates to avoid any problems with credit/debit card use overseas. ATMs are plentiful, and credit cards are readily accepted in cities, but it's a good idea to keep some local cash on hand, especially in more remote places.
When traveling to Turkey in 2024, you need to know where to exchange your cash for Turkish Lira (TRY). The local currency is generally accepted, and there are several choices for currency conversion in significant locations:

Airports: Major international airports, such as Istanbul Atatürk Airport and Istanbul Airport, feature currency exchange facilities where you may convert your cash to Turkish Lira. These services are often offered at both the arrival and departure zones.

Banks: Banks all around Turkey provide currency exchange services. Most banks are open during business hours on weekdays, with some branches in tourist regions offering longer hours.

Currency Exchange Offices:

Independent currency exchange offices, or "döviz bürosu," are common in tourist regions, commercial districts, and city centers. They frequently provide affordable pricing and flexible operation hours.

Hotels and resorts:

Many hotels and resorts in tourist destinations provide currency exchange services for the convenience of their customers. While the prices may not be as competitive as those at independent exchange offices, they are a convenient choice.

ATMs (automated teller machines):

ATMs are extensively distributed across Turkey, including in small villages. They provide a handy option to withdraw Turkish Lira with your international debit or credit card. Make sure your bank is informed of your travel dates to avoid any problems with card usage overseas.

Credit Card Usage:

Hotels, restaurants, and stores often accept credit cards, particularly in metropolitan regions. However, it is recommended to carry some cash for purchases at more rural or smaller places.

Online Currency Exchange Platforms:

Online currency exchange companies allow you to order Turkish Lira in advance and have it delivered to your home or picked up at designated places. Examine the dependability and prices connected with these services.

When converting currencies, always compare rates and fees to ensure you are getting the greatest value. Furthermore, be aware of your safety and only utilize recognized money exchange services in Turkey.

Description of clothes to wear and there classification

To respect Turkish culture, learn about local customs and etiquette. In mosques, modest clothing is required, and women frequently cover their heads. When entering a home, it is traditional to take off your shoes. Bargaining is typical at marketplaces, so feel free to haggle

Traditional and Modern Dress in Turkey Travel Guide 2024:

1. **Traditional Turkish attire**:
Men's Clothing: Shalvar (Baggy pants):
Loose-fitting pants typically paired with a traditional tunic.
Fes (Hat): A cylindrical felt hat customarily ornamented with a tassel.
Yelek (Vest): Embroidered vests worn over tunics on special occasions.
Women's Clothing: Kaftans are long, flowing robes with complex designs.
Tesettür: Many ladies wear a traditional headscarf that covers their hair and neck.
2. **Contemporary Urban Wear**:
Turkish men frequently wear contemporary suits in metropolitan settings, reflecting worldwide fashion trends.
Casual attire includes jeans, t-shirts, and shirts.
Turkish ladies enjoy modern fashion, such as dresses and skirts.
Headscarves: While not required, some women like to wear them, and current fashions incorporate them smoothly into elegant attire.

3. **Beach and Resort Wears**: Swimwear is common throughout the shore, with beachgoers wearing bikinis and swim trunks.
Light Cover-Ups: Loose-fitting cover-ups and kaftans are ideal for going from the beach to another activity.
4. **Religious attire:** Islamic Modest Wear: Some people adhere to Islamic customs by wearing more modest clothing, such as long-sleeved shirts and conservative gowns.
Some men wear kufis (skullcaps) as religious and cultural symbols.

5. **Seasonal Variation**:

Winter Attire: Warm clothing, jackets, and scarves are used throughout the colder months, particularly in the central and eastern areas.
Summer Clothing: Lightweight textiles like cotton and linen are favored throughout the sunny summer months.

6. **Festive and special occasion attire:**

Henna Nightgowns: For pre-wedding events, women may wear beautiful Henna Nightgowns in brilliant hues.
Formal occasions are generally attended in traditional clothing, with ladies wearing magnificent evening gowns.

Turkey's clothing spectrum is a colorful blend of history and modernity, with numerous styles representing the country's rich cultural background as well as contemporary inspirations in 2024.

weather and ideal time to travel

Consider the ideal time to visit based on your preferences. Spring (April to June) and fall (September to November) provide ideal weather for seeing historical sites and natural marvels. Summer (July to August) draws beachgoers, while winter (December to February) is perfect for winter sports enthusiasts in areas such as Cappadocia.

Transportation

Turkey has a robust transportation network. Domestic aircraft are effective for long-distance travel, whilst buses and railroads are dependable for shorter trips. Public transit in cities is easy, but hiring a car provides greater freedom, particularly in rural regions.

Transportation and the price range and standard Service Provided: City and intercity transportation. Price Range: Reasonable, with costs normally determined by distance.

Availability: Widely available in both urban and suburban locations.

2. **Shared Taxis (Dolmuş):**

Service Provided: Shared taxi services for short to medium distances.

Price Range: Economical, providing an affordable alternative to private cabs.

Availability: Common in cities and tourist destinations.

3. Metro and trams:

Service Provided: Urban train transit in major cities.

Price Range: Relatively inexpensive for a handy and efficient form of transportation.

Availability: Found in large cities such as Istanbul and Ankara.

4. **Ferry and Boats**:

Service Provided: Intercontinental and local boat services.

Price range: Affordable, particularly for shorter boat journeys.

Availability: Most prevalent in coastal cities and areas.

5. **Domestic flights**:

Service Provided: Air travel between major cities and tourist locations.

Budget airlines provide affordable fares for domestic flights.

Availability: Frequent flights link significant destinations.

6. Intercity buses:

Service Provided: Long-distance travel between cities.

The price range varies depending on distance and bus class (regular, business, or VIP).

Availability: The network is extensive and covers the whole country.

7. **Car Rental**:

Service Provided: Rental automobiles for personal exploring.

Price Range: Affordable, with alternatives for many automobile kinds.

Availability: Available in major airports and metropolitan areas.

8. Shared rides:
Ride-sharing applications are used to carpool and share trips.
Price Range: Affordable for short to medium distances.
Availability: Common in big cities.

9. Bicycle rental:
Service Provided: Bike rentals for urban and picturesque adventure.
Price range: Low daily or hourly prices.
Availability: Primarily in metropolitan regions and tourist hot places.

10. Walking tour:
Service Provided: Guided walking tours for sightseeing.
Price range: Reasonable, with possibilities for group or private tours.
Availability: Common in historic and cultural districts.

Before making any transportation plans, compare costs, read reviews, and select the one that best fits your budget and travel needs. Prices may vary depending on the season, location, and service provider

Istanbul:

Public buses: Istanbul has a large and reasonably priced public bus network that provides inexpensive transit around the city.

Dolmuş Stations: Shared taxis (Dolmuş) run from a variety of stations, providing affordable trips for short distances.

Ankara:

Ankara's well-developed metro and bus networks give cost-effective transportation choices for exploring the capital.

Izmir:

The İzmir Suburban System (İZBAN) provides cheap rail services between suburban communities and the city center.

Ferry Terminals: In coastal cities such as Izmir, ferries provide inexpensive transit between areas.

Antalya:

Antalya's tram system and public buses provide economical transit, particularly within the city.

Adana:

Adana's public transportation system comprises buses and minibusses, providing affordable choices for moving about the city.

Bursa:
Bursaray: Bursa's metro system, Bursaray, offers affordable transit choices to both inhabitants and visitors.
Gaziantep:
Gaziantep's public bus system provides affordable options to explore the city and its surroundings.
Kayseri:
Kayseray is Kayseri's tram system, which provides economical and efficient city transit.
Trabzon:
Minibuses and shared taxis (Dolmuş) are widely utilized in Trabzon, providing affordable choices for short-distance transport.
Eskişehir:
Eskişehir's tram system and local buses provide affordable transportation for both residents and visitors.

budget friendly transportation,standard location and recommendation Transportation choices with anticipated price ranges, locations, and suggestions in various regions of Turkey for the Turkey Travel Guide 2024:

Istanbul Urban Mobility: Metro and Trams

Price range: Low

Recommendation: Istanbul's metro and tram systems are efficient and cost-effective, connecting key sites. Use the Istanbulkart for easy fare payments.

Ferry across the Bosporus

Price range: moderate.

Recommendation: Take a picturesque Bosphorus trip on public boats. Depart from Eminönü for spectacular views of the city.

Interstate Travel: Highways and buses

Intercity Buses

Price range: low to moderate.

Recommendation: For pleasant and cheap interstate travel, choose reliable bus operators like Metro Turizm and Kamil Koç.

Car Rentals

Prices range from moderate to high.

Renting a car allows you greater freedom, especially when visiting places like Cappadocia or the Aegean

Coast. Major vehicle rental companies have locations at airports and major centers.
Cappadocia Exploration: Hot Air Balloon Rides Price range: High Recommendation: Experience Cappadocia's enchanting chimneys at dawn with a hot air balloon flight. Companies such as Voyager Balloons provide amazing experiences.

ATV Tours

Price range: moderate.

Recommendation: Take an ATV journey through Cappadocia's diverse landscapes. Local providers, such as ATV Goreme, offer interesting adventures. Coastal transportation in Antalya includes trams and public buses.

Price range: low to moderate.

Recommendation: Antalya's excellent tram and bus systems make around the city and visiting adjacent sights easy and economical.

Dolmus Services

Price range: Low Recommendation: For short journeys, use dolmus services (shared minibusses) on fixed routes throughout Antalya and adjacent areas.

These transportation choices meet the unique demands of passengers from various regions of

Turkey. Prices may vary depending on distance, vehicle type, and travel preferences. It is best to verify with the appropriate transportation companies for the most up-to-date pricing and availability. When visiting these Turkish locations, try combining these low-cost transportation choices to save money on your trip. Always check the most recent timetables and itineraries to find the most cost-effective and efficient forms of transportation.To ensure safety, stay up-to-date on current travel warnings for Turkey. Take standard safety precautions, remain alert of your surroundings, and keep your possessions secure. Emergency services, including medical facilities, are offered in major cities.

By addressing these travel logistics and necessities, you'll establish the framework for a seamless and pleasurable journey across Turkey in 2024. Check for changes and further recommendations closer to your vacation dates.

CHAPTER THREE

Top Destinations

Turkey, a country straddling two continents, entices visitors with a variety of interesting places that combine history, culture, and natural beauty. The Hagia Sophia, located in the center of Istanbul, is a symbol of Byzantine and Ottoman grandeur. The Blue Mosque, with its beautiful tiles, and the bustling Grand Bazaar immerse tourists in this city' complex fabric of East and West.

Cappadocia, a magical wonderland in central Turkey, captivates visitors with its fanciful landscapes of fairy chimneys and cave homes. Hot air balloon excursions provide stunning views, making them a must-see for visitors seeking enchantment.

Ephesus, located on the Aegean shore, displays its ancient riches. The Library of Celsus and the Great Theatre take tourists to the height of the Roman Empire, providing a historical voyage through this ancient city.

Pamukkale, often known as the "Cotton Castle," has cascading terraces of mineral-rich hot springs against a backdrop of ancient ruins. The strange

terrain of southern Turkey promotes leisure and exploration.
Antalya, located along the Mediterranean coast, is enticed by its crystal-clear seas and ancient charm. The ancient town, Kaleiçi, welcomes strolls along cobblestone lanes and Ottoman-era buildings.
The ancient city of Troy, buried in myth, rests in the northwest area, beckoning tourists to discover its archeological wonders and mythical stories.
Turkey's capital, Ankara, combines modernism with tradition. The Atatürk Mausoleum and the Museum of Anatolian Civilizations offer insight into the country's origins and rich history.
Mount Ararat and Mount Nemrut have unique landscapes that lure visitors to uncover natural and archeological wonders.
As you travel through these top sites, the Turkey Travel Guide 2024 tells a timeless story, encouraging you to behold the splendors of ancient civilizations, enjoy the aromas of different landscapes, and immerse yourself in the warm embrace of Turkish hospitality. Each site exposes a distinct chapter, resulting in a voyage that combines the echoes of history with the energy of the present.

Istanbul: Bridging East and West

Istanbul, a metropolis that spans two continents, serves as a bustling bridge between East and West, providing a captivating combination of history, culture, and modernity. The Hagia Sophia, located in the center of this busy metropolis, is an architectural marvel that reflects the city's Byzantine origins and later transitions into an Ottoman masterpiece. Its huge dome and elaborate mosaics evoke stories of civilizations that have left an everlasting stamp on the local skyline.

The Blue Mosque, located next to the Hagia Sophia, enchants visitors with its magnificent minarets and sea of blue tiles, a harmonious representation of the city's religious and cultural diversity. The Grand Bazaar, one of the world's oldest and biggest covered markets, immerses visitors in a kaleidoscope of colors, fragrances, and noises that reflect centuries of trade and artistry.

As the Bosphorus Strait separates Istanbul between Europe and Asia, the city's shoreline is alive with the silhouettes of stately palaces such as the famed Topkapi Palace and the Dolmabahçe Palace. Bosphorus cruises provide a unique perspective, allowing visitors to see the harmonious mix of old sites and modern structures.

Taksim Square and Beyoğlu, home to contemporary art galleries, stylish boutiques, and energetic nightlife, are pulsating hubs of modern Istanbul. The Galata Tower, which has stood tall since medieval times, offers panoramic views of the city, encouraging tourists to see Istanbul's ever-changing cityscape.
Istanbul in 2024 invites visitors to discover its many districts, experience the aromas of its culinary pleasures, and immerse themselves in the rhythm of a city that seamlessly combines the old and the contemporary. Whether exploring the complex passageways of the Grand Bazaar or admiring the city's silhouette from a Bosphorus boat, Istanbul exemplifies the beautiful junction of East and West.

Cappadocia: Fairy chimneys and cave dwellings

Cappadocia, located in the heart of central Turkey, is a magical environment that defies expectations. This location is well-known for its surreal allure, with fairy chimneys, cave homes, and ethereal panoramas that transport visitors to a dreamscape.
The characteristic fairy chimneys, towering spires of soft volcanic rock carved by centuries of erosion,

form a bizarre background against the Cappadocian sky. These fanciful structures act as sentinels, encouraging investigation and captivating the imaginations of those who are lucky enough to experience their particular attraction.
Cave houses, cut from the fragile tuff rock, tell a story of ancient living. The troglodyte architecture, which includes homes, churches, and entire towns concealed under the rock formations, adds a magical element to Cappadocia's ancient tapestry. Göreme Open-Air Museum, a UNESCO World Heritage site, displays a collection of rock-cut chapels embellished with magnificent paintings, offering a look into the region's rich Byzantine history.
One of the most memorable ways to see Cappadocia is from above. Hot air balloon tours before dawn reveal the true beauty of the country, as multicolored balloons smoothly soar over the fairy chimneys, revealing valleys and vineyards underneath. It's a fascinating and unforgettable way to see the wonders of Cappadocia.
Exploring old underground civilizations like Derinkuyu and Kaymaklı lends a mystery element to the experience. These underground structures, carved out of soft rock, were formerly used as

hiding places for early Christians fleeing persecution.
In 2024, Cappadocia will welcome visitors to experience its surreal beauty and explore the ancient echoes etched in its cave houses and fairy chimneys. Whether soaring above in a hot air balloon or wandering through subterranean passages, Cappadocia offers an immersive experience that defies the limits of imagination and reality.

Ephesus: Ancient ruins and historical marvels

Ephesus, an archaeological gem in western Turkey, reveals its ancient grandeur via a tapestry of ruins that transports tourists back in time. This city, steeped in history, was once a thriving Roman metropolis, and its well-preserved relics now provide a compelling voyage into classical antiquity. The Library of Celsus is an iconic emblem of Ephesus, showcasing architectural beauty and intellectual power. Its façade, embellished with beautiful figures and reliefs, formerly contained thousands of scrolls and served as a light of knowledge in ancient times. Today, tourists marvel at the relics of this magnificent library, envisioning the intellectual zeal that once filled its halls.

The Great Theatre, an enormous amphitheater, vibrates with the sounds of old performances. It had a seating capacity of 25,000 and hosted gladiatorial bouts, theater plays, and public meetings. Standing in the middle of Ephesus, the theater offers a magnificent perspective of the surrounding countryside.

Walking through the old marble-paved alleys, travelers come across the Temple of Artemis, one of the Seven Wonders of the Old World. While only parts exist, its historical value is undeniable. The Terrace Houses, which include magnificently preserved paintings, provide an insight into the lavish lifestyle of Ephesus' aristocracy.

In 2024, Ephesus welcomes visitors to walk its stone-paved streets, touch the aged columns of its temples, and immerse themselves in the grandeur of a city that once represented the cultural and architectural pinnacle of the Roman Empire. With each step, Ephesus tells a story of magnificence, exposing the layers of its rich history and leaving an unforgettable mark on those who enter its ancient embrace.

CHAPTER FOUR

Culinary Delights

Turkey's culinary scene is a delightful voyage that tantalizes the taste senses with a complex tapestry of tastes that seamlessly merge history and innovation. In 2024, the Turkey Travel Guide will host a gourmet excursion to commemorate the country's unique culinary legacy.

Enjoy Turkish kebabs, marinated and cooked to perfection. on the classic Döner Kebab, finely cut on a spinning vertical spit, to the delicious Adana Kebab, rich in spices, every taste is a culinary treat. Discover the world of mezes, a delicious collection of tiny delicacies that accompany meals. Hummus, eggplant salads, and stuffed grape leaves highlight the bright tastes of Turkish appetizers. For a really genuine experience, serve them with traditional Turkish tea or coffee.

Baklava, a thin pastry filled with nuts and sweetened with honey or syrup, is a delicious sweet treat. Lokum, or Turkish pleasure, is a wonderful selection

of chewy confections in a variety of flavors, including rose and pomegranate.
Coastal locations provide delicious seafood from the Mediterranean and Aegean oceans. Grilled fish, calamari, and octopus are seasoned with herbs and spices, providing a sense of the sea's freshness.
Start the day with a Turkish breakfast buffet with cheeses, olives, tomatoes, cucumbers, and freshly baked bread. Menemen, a dish of eggs, tomatoes, and green peppers, gives a substantial element to the morning meal.

Manti & Pide: Delicious Turkish dumplings filled with spicy meat or lentils, topped with garlic yogurt and red pepper-infused butter. Pide, a Turkish flatbread that is sometimes compared to pizza, comes in a variety of toppings and shapes.
As you explore Turkey's culinary environment in 2024, let the flavors of its different dishes guide you, resulting in a symphony of tastes that reflect the country's rich cultural mosaic. Every eating experience in Turkey, from crowded markets to tiny local cafes, takes you on a trip through the country's culinary heritage.
In Turkey, enjoying excellent and economical culinary experiences is part of the journey. For

budget-conscious tourists in 2024, here are a few spots where you may enjoy local pleasures without breaking the bank:

1. **Street Food Stalls**: Explore the bustling street food scene for affordable alternatives including Simit (sesame-crusted bread rings), Kumpir (stuffed baked potatoes), and Döner Kebabs. Street sellers frequently provide quick, good meals at low costs.

2. **smaller Markets and Bazaars**: Explore vibrant markets like the Grand Bazaar in Istanbul or smaller markets in other towns. These markets not only sell fresh produce but also feature food vendors that serve economical and authentic cuisine. Try Gözleme (thin Turkish flatbread with varied fillings) and Börek (savory pastries) from market sellers.

3. **Lokantas (Local Restaurants)**: These traditional Turkish eateries provide home-style cuisine at moderate costs. These eateries cater to locals, serving substantial dishes such as Kuru Fasulye (white bean stew) and Tavuklu Pilav (chicken pilaf).

4. **Çay Bahçesis (Tea Gardens)**: Enjoy Turkish tea or coffee and small appetizers at these charming tea

gardens. These places frequently have a relaxing environment, and you may accompany your tea with inexpensive pastries or simit.

5. **Look for neighborhood kebab** businesses away from tourist areas. These modest businesses frequently serve inexpensive kebabs, dürüm (wraps), and pide (Turkish flatbread with toppings).

6. **Student Districts**: Eateries in university or student districts provide budget-friendly meals. These restaurants serve a variety of cuisines at reasonable prices for students.

7. **Fast Food Options**: Turkish fast-food businesses like Tarihi Sultanahmet Köftecisi and Pideban offer quick and economical meals. You may have köfte (meatballs) and pide (Turkish pizza) at moderate prices.
Remember that the finest gastronomic experiences are typically found by visiting local spots and connecting with pleasant locals. Don't be afraid to ask for ideas or try something new; Turkey's diversified cuisine scene has something for every bud

In Turkey, enjoying excellent and economical culinary experiences is part of the journey. For budget-conscious tourists in 2024, here are a few spots where you may enjoy local pleasures without breaking the ban

Turkish cuisine highlights

In 2024, embark on a gastronomic tour around Turkey, where you will discover bright tastes, fragrant spices, and a complex tapestry of cuisine reflecting the country's many cultural influences. Turkish cuisine, from street food vendors to classic restaurants, is a culinary treat that creates an indelible memory.

1. **Kebabs**: Turkish kebabs are famous for their juicy meats marinated in herbs and spices and cooked to perfection. Döner Kebab, a traditional street meal, has thinly sliced slices of meat rotating on a vertical spit, which is frequently served on flatbread with fresh vegetables and sauce.

2. **Start the day with a Turkish breakfast of cheeses, olives,** tomatoes, cucumbers, and freshly baked bread. Hummus, Baba Ganoush, and Dolma are examples of mezes or small appetizers.

3. **Baklava and Turkish Delight**: Treat your sweet craving with layers of thin pastry packed with chopped nuts and sweetened with honey or syrup. Turkish pleasure, also known as Lokum, is a type of chewy treat that comes in a variety of flavors and is sometimes coated with powdered sugar or coconut.

4. **Pide and Lahmacun**: Enjoy the taste of Pide, a boat-shaped Turkish flatbread topped with a variety of toppings like pizza. Lahmacun, also known as Turkish pizza, has a thin crust covered with minced meat, veggies, and spices.

5. **Turkish Tea and Coffee:** Explore Turkish tea culture, where strong black tea is served in tiny cups, surrounded by discussion and warmth. Turkish coffee, finely ground and unfiltered, has a strong caffeine rush and is typically served with a piece of Turkish delight.

6. **Manti and Kuzu Tandir:** Enjoy the delicious flavor of Manti, which are little dumplings filled with spiced meat or lentils, topped with garlic yogurt, and drizzled with red pepper-infused butter. Kuzu Tandir, slow-cooked lamb, is a mouthwatering meal seasoned with fragrant herbs.

In 2024, Turkish cuisine encourages you to discover its unique culinary legacy, with each dish telling a narrative about the country's history and cultural mix. Whether dining at a local restaurant, eating street cuisine or sipping tea in a historic tea garden, each culinary experience celebrates the tastes that constitute Turkey's gastronomic identity.

Must-try dishes and local eateries

Take a gastronomic journey around Turkey and enjoy a variety of flavors at these must-try local restaurants, where each dish tells a narrative about heritage and taste.

1. **Tarihi Sultanahmet Köftecisi** (Istanbul): Enjoy the artistic kebabs at this popular diner in Istanbul. Try the Köfte, which are tasty Turkish meatballs seasoned with spices and served with grilled veggies.
2. **Halil Lahmacun (Antakya)** serves true Lahmacun, a Turkish pizza with a thin crust covered with minced meat, onions, and spices. It's a delicious snack that's ideal for sharing.
3. **Karaköy Lokantası (Istanbul**) offers delicious mezes. Dive into a range of Hummus, Babaganoush, and other appetizers that highlight the vast diversity of Turkish tastes.
4. **Fish Sandwiches at Karaköy Balıkçısı (Istanbul):** Experience Istanbul's seafood scene at this restaurant. Enjoy a freshly grilled fish sandwich, a typical street snack on the Bosphorus.
5. **Mantarli Tavuk Sarma at Çiya Sofrası (Istanbul):** This Istanbul restaurant is a gastronomic marvel. Try Mantarli Tavuk Sarma, a dish with chicken covered in mushrooms and grape leaves that

different taste the restaurant's dedication to traditional Turkish cuisine.

6. **Bursa Kebapçısı (Bursa**): For those who love döner kebab, Bursa Kebapçısı is the place to go. Enjoy a traditional Döner wrap filled with properly seasoned pork, fresh veggies, and a drizzle of sauce.

7. **Iskender at Kebapçı İskender (Bursa):** Kebapçı İskender in Bursa is famous for its Iskender meal, which consists of sliced döner beef, yogurt, and tomato sauce over pide pieces.

8. **Ali Baba Kebapçısı** offers a one-of-a-kind Testi Kebab experience in Cappadocia. This recipe has slow-cooked beef and veggies wrapped in a clay pot, resulting in a luscious and savory masterpiece.

Meşhur Mantıci Murat Bozok in Ankara is famous for its Manti, which are little dumplings filled with spicy meat or lentils and topped with yogurt and garlic-infused butter.

10. **Van Kahvaltı Evi (Van)** offers an excellent Turkish breakfast. Indulge in a selection of cheeses, olives, honey, and other delicacies that highlight the region's unique tastes.

Allow your taste sensations to guide you through these local restaurants in 2024, where the essence of Turkish food is shown with each bite. Each dish is a culinary marvel that takes you back to this enchanting country's rich gastronomic tradition

Restaurant recommendations , including projected price ranges, locations, and attractions in several regions of Turkey:

Istanbul Gastronomic Delights: **1. Nusr-Et Steakhouse, Nişantaşı

Cuisine: Turkish steakhouse.

Price Range: High Recommendation: Enjoy fine pieces of meat cooked with flair by globally acclaimed chef Nusret Gökçe, often known as "Salt Bae."

2**. Mikla, Beyoğlu.**

Cuisine: modern Turkish.

Price Range: High.

Recommendation: Mikla offers a great dining experience with spectacular views of Istanbul. Chef Mehmet Gürs blends Turkish and Scandinavian cuisine.

Coastal Culinary Delights in Antalya: **1. Can Can Pide, Kaleiçi

Cuisine: Turkish Pizza (Pide)

Price range: moderate.

Recommendation: Enjoy classic Turkish pide with numerous toppings in the picturesque surroundings of Kaleiçi.2. Vanilla Lounge, Lara Beach.

Cuisine: international.

Prices range from moderate to high.

Recommendation: Indulge in a broad cuisine at Vanilla Lounge, which serves foreign and Turkish delicacies and overlooks the Mediterranean.

Cappadocian Dining Experience: 1. Dibek Restaurant, Göreme.

Cuisine: Turkish Price: Moderate

Recommendation: Dibek, noted for its traditional clay pot-cooked meals, offers authentic Cappadocian food in a quiet atmosphere.

2. Seki Restaurant, Ortahisar.

Cuisine: Anatolian.

Price range: moderate.

Recommendation: Experience local delicacies at Seki Restaurant, located in a historic structure in Ortahisar, affording panoramic views of the countryside.

These restaurant choices reflect the gastronomic diversity found in Turkey. Prices may vary depending on menu selection and eating preference. It is best to contact the restaurants directly for themost up-to-date prices and to book appointments, particularly for popular businesses.

CHAPTER FIVE

Outdoor Adventures

Turkey's various landscapes offer a playground for outdoor lovers looking for adventurous adventures in 2024. Cappadocia, with its strange rock formations, welcomes hot air balloon trips before dawn, providing a stunning view of fairy chimneys and cave homes. The region's distinctive landscape is ideal for thrilling treks and off-road adventures. The Lycian Way, which runs along the Mediterranean coast, invites hikers to follow ancient trails that lead to stunning vistas of turquoise seas and historic sites. The Turkish Riviera is ideal for scuba diving, with opportunities to explore diverse underwater ecosystems and old shipwrecks.

For an adrenaline rush, head to the Kaçkar Mountains, where you can go rock climbing, paragliding, or mountaineering. The Saklikent Gorge in Fethiye offers an exciting challenge for canyoning aficionados as they navigate through breathtaking natural gorges.

Adventurers can also try white-water rafting on the Köprülü River or take a hot air balloon flight over Pamukkale's strange surroundings. Whether traversing historic pathways, swimming into crystal-clear seas, or soaring over breathtaking terrains, Turkey's outdoor experiences in 2024 guarantee an amazing combination of nature, culture, and adrenaline.

Hot air ballooning in Cappadocia

Take an unforgettable ride over the breathtaking scenery of Cappadocia with the exciting sensation of hot air ballooning. According to Turkey Travel Guide 2023, the appeal of Cappadocia's fairy chimneys and distinctive rock formations takes on a mystical dimension when you soar in a multicolored hot air balloon at dawn.

Drifting effortlessly across the ethereal environment, you'll see the sunshine its first light on the bizarre terrain, producing a kaleidoscope of hues that dance across the old rocks below. The surreal vista emerges as you glide over valleys, vineyards, and ancient landmarks, giving you a bird's-eye perspective of Cappadocia's incomparable splendor. The experience is not only exhilarating but also calm and awe-inspiring, allowing you to enjoy the region's natural treasures from a unique viewpoint. As the hot air balloon floats softly, your senses are heightened, and the calm of the moment contrasts with the amazing vistas, generating memories that will last long after the descent. Hot air ballooning in Cappadocia is a must-do activity, providing a one-of-a-kind and unforgettable opportunity to experience the bewitching spirit of this intriguing area in Turkey.

Coastal escapes and water activities

Turkey's coastal retreats entice tourists in 2024 with a symphony of turquoise waters, beautiful beaches, and a wealth of aquatic activities catering to both sunbathers and adventurers. The Lycian Way winds across the Turkish Riviera, presenting secret coves, ancient ruins, and stunning seascapes. This seaside hiking path beckons investigation, providing an ideal balance of visual beauty and historical mystery.

The Mediterranean and Aegean shores provide a playground for water activities. The crystal-clear seas around Fethiye are suitable for scuba diving, revealing lively underwater worlds and hidden antiquities from centuries ago. Snorkeling aficionados can see a variety of marine life along the beaches of Kas and Kalkan.

The Kaş-Kekova route provides an amazing sailing experience, taking you past the submerged city of Simena and immersing you in the charm of isolated bays. Chartering a traditional Turkish gulet is a wonderful way to see the coastline's hidden beauties. Thrill-seekers may go white-water rafting on the Köprülü River, negotiating spectacular rapids against a backdrop of gorgeous scenery. Paragliding over the picturesque Ölüdeniz lagoon adds an adrenaline-pumping dimension to seaside excursions, affording panoramic views of the calm Blue Lagoon and surrounding hills.

Windsurfers may ride the Aegean winds at Alacati, making it a popular water sports destination. The combination of natural beauty, historical landmarks, and a wide range of water sports along Turkey's beaches offers an enticing draw for visitors looking for the ideal seaside getaway in 2024. Whether you want to relax on sun-kissed beaches or get an adrenaline rush on the water, Turkey's coastal areas provide a diverse and unique playground for all types of traveler

CHAPTER SIX

Historical Landmarks

Immerse yourself in the rich tapestry of history that has been woven into the country's very fabric with the Turkey Travel Guide 2024. Istanbul, the city where East meets West, is home to the magnificent Hagia Sophia, a symbol of Byzantine and Ottoman grandeur, as well as the Blue Mosque, an architectural masterpiece decorated with exquisite tiles. The Topkapi Palace, originally the seat of Ottoman sultans, now houses sumptuous rooms and treasury treasures.

Ephesus, an archeological treasure, reveals its historical magnificence through the Library of Celsus and the Great Theatre, where echoes of ancient Roman life resound. Troy, cloaked in myth, welcomes investigation of its ancient remains and mythical stories.

The strange landscapes of Cappadocia are peppered with ancient sites, including the Göreme Open-Air Museum, which has rock-cut churches embellished with Byzantine murals. Mount Nemrut, with its massive monuments and old graves, bears witness to a once-mighty monarchy.

The ancient remains along the Lycian Way, such as Xanthos and Letoon, take you back to a time when Lycian towns flourished. As you travel around Turkey's historical sites in 2024, each location tells a story of civilization, letting you follow in the footsteps of emperors, sultans, and ancient cultures that have left an everlasting impact on this enthralling region.

Hagia Sophia and Blue Mosque in Istanbul

The Hagia Sophia and Blue Mosque, located in the center of Istanbul, are emblematic icons of the city's historical and architectural beauty, enticing visitors to see the centuries-long confluence of civilizations. The Hagia Sophia, which dates back to the sixth century, was once a Byzantine cathedral before becoming an Ottoman mosque and now a museum. Its gigantic dome, rich mosaics, and magnificent architecture evoke Byzantine grandeur, repeating stories of emperors that molded Istanbul's skyline. **The Blue Mosque**, also known as Sultan Ahmed Mosque, is adjacent to the Hagia Sophia and captivates visitors with its magnificent domes and minarets. The mosque, adorned with approximately 20,000 blue tiles that give it its name, is an Ottoman

architectural gem. Inside, a spacious prayer room has a remarkable combination of light and space, providing a peaceful mood.
Visitors to Istanbul can tour these ancient buildings in 2024, marveling at the sublime beauty of the Hagia Sophia and the Blue Mosque's exquisite combination of Islamic and Byzantine influences, respectively. Together, they constitute an enthralling team, capturing the city's rich cultural and religious past that has survived centuries of mutation and adaptation

Ancient wonders of Troy and Ephesus

Travel through time to Turkey's archeological treasures of Troy and Ephesus, where vestiges of ancient civilizations tell fascinating stories. Troy, immortalized in Homer's epics, displays layers of history through its archeological site. Explore the recreated wooden horse and the city's historic walls, following in the footsteps of famous heroes and viewing the remnants of a city that once stood at the crossroads of East and West.

Ephesus, an antique treasure, encourages visitors to immerse themselves in ancient Roman culture. The Library of Celsus, an architectural masterpiece, exemplifies wisdom and majesty. The Great Theatre, where St. Paul once lectured, evokes the grandeur of Roman life. Wander through marble-paved lanes lined with columns to see the Temple of Artemis, one of the Seven Wonders of the Ancient World.

According to Turkey Travel Guide 2024, these historic monuments offer a physical connection to the past, letting tourists imagine the vivid lives and sophisticated civilizations that once thrived on these sacred land

CHAPTER SEVEN

Cultural Experiences

Immerse yourself in a tapestry of cultural encounters that reveal Turkey's unique essence. Istanbul, the dynamic bridge between continents, welcomes you to visit the Grand Bazaar, a maze of busy merchants selling spices, fabrics, and artisan items. The city's historic neighborhoods, including Sultanahmet and Beyoğlu, showcase Ottoman and current Turkish culture.

Beyond Istanbul, discover the genuine beauty of the Turkish countryside, where individuals open their homes to enjoy traditional foods and stories. Participate in a traditional Turkish tea ceremony, enjoying the hospitality with each cup.

Witness the mysterious whirling dervishes perform the Sufi dance, which is a captivating representation of spirituality and cultural heritage. Attend festivals that showcase Turkey's rich cultural variety, such as the International Istanbul Film Festival and traditional music events.

Art lovers may visit galleries in Ankara and Izmir, while history aficionados can discover the stories of ancient monuments like Ephesus and Troy. Turkey in 2024 promises a cultural journey in which each step is an invitation to interact with the diversity of cultures, languages, and rituals that create this vibrant

Traditional Turkish baths (Hamams)

Turkish baths, or hamams, are central to Turkey's cultural experience, bringing together history, leisure, and pleasure. Immerse yourself in the age-old custom of hamams, which is an essential element of Turkish culture, with the Turkey Travel Guide 2024.

Step into a relaxing atmosphere filled with beautiful tiles and marble surfaces that represent the luxury of Ottoman style. Begin your adventure with a warm-up in the steam room, where the moderate heat prepares your body for the ancient bathing routine.

Experience a rigorous scrub performed by professional attendants using a traditional kese

(exfoliating glove), revealing silky-smooth skin. The following step is a delightful foam massage, in which aromatic soap bubbles surround you in a fragrant hug.
The marble-slabbed heated platform is the focal point of many hamams, creating a tranquil environment for relaxation. Allow centuries of history to wash over you while you relax, instilling a sense of renewal and peace.
With hamams dispersed across Istanbul and beyond, each has its own distinct beauty. From ancient sites like the Çemberlitaş Hamamı to modern interpretations, these cultural sanctuaries enable you to rest in an environment that effortlessly integrates the past with contemporary wellness. In 2024, let the timeless charm of Turkish baths transport you to a world where pleasure meets tradition.

Whirling Dervishes and Sufi traditions

Witness the mesmerizing ritual of the Whirling Dervishes, an old Sufi custom that goes beyond dancing to become a spiritual experience, as described in Turkey Travel Guide 2024. This

captivating event, based on the mystical teachings of Sufi poet Rumi, takes place in locations such as Konya, where the Mevlevi Order preserves a centuries-old tradition.
The Whirling Dervishes, dressed in flowing white robes and towering headgear, perform the beautiful dance known as the Sema. The dancers twirl in tandem, symbolizing spiritual elevation, their revolutions representing the celestial voyage toward divine love. The accompanying music, a combination of traditional instruments and chants, heightens the contemplative atmosphere.
Attending a Whirling Dervish ritual provides tourists in 2024 with a deep understanding of Sufi philosophy. It's not only a show, but a spiritual exercise in which repeated motions induce a trance, allowing practitioners to connect with the holy.
This Sufi tradition acts as a link between the terrestrial and celestial realms, encouraging viewers to see a holy dance that spans time. The Whirling Dervishes' captivating embrace reveals Turkey's spiritual legacy, providing a transforming experience that lasts long after the final spin comes to a graceful

CHAPTER EIGHT

Entertainment and Festivals

THE Turkey Travel Guide 2024, the vibrant tapestry of Turkish culture is interwoven with a rich array of entertainment and festivals, showcasing the nation's zest for life and celebration. Istanbul, a city pulsating with energy, hosts numerous cultural events throughout the year. The International Istanbul Film Festival attracts cinephiles, bringing together filmmakers and enthusiasts for a cinematic extravaganza.

Festival-goers can immerse themselves in the Istanbul Jazz Festival, where international and local artists converge to create an electrifying ambiance across the city's historic venues. The Istanbul Music Festival, featuring classical and contemporary performances, adds a melodic touch to the cultural calendar.

Beyond Istanbul, regional festivals offer a glimpse into diverse traditions. The Mevlana Whirling Dervishes Festival in Konya honors the mystical teachings of Rumi with mesmerizing Sufi rituals. In the Aegean town of Ephesus, the Artemis Festival

celebrates ancient cultures through music and dance against the backdrop of historic ruins.
In 2024, immerse yourself in Turkey's festive spirit, where each event becomes a window into the nation's dynamic cultural mosaic. From music and film to ancient rituals, the entertainment scene in Turkey promises an unforgettable blend of modern vivacity and timeless traditions.

Cultural events and festivals

The Turkey Travel Guide 2024 encourages you to participate in a kaleidoscope of cultural events and festivals that highlight the unique traditions of this enchanting country. Istanbul, a cultural hub, presents the foreign Istanbul Film Festival, which draws cinephiles from all over the world to enjoy a cinematic celebration of both local and foreign films.
For music fans, the Istanbul Jazz Festival transforms the city into a melodious paradise, pulsating with the various sounds of jazz musicians. The Istanbul Music Festival, which features a harmonic combination of classical and contemporary acts, contributes to the city's cultural fabric.

Travel outside of the bustling metropolis to enjoy rural festivals. The Ephesus Artemis Festival, set against the backdrop of ancient ruins, features vivid music and dance that celebrates the Aegean region's cultural heritage. The Mevlana Whirling Dervishes Festival in Konya celebrates Sufi mysticism with captivating rituals and dances.
Whether you find yourself in the ancient atmosphere of Istanbul or immersed in the cultural traditions of provincial festivals, Turkey in 2024 promises a plethora of activities that blend modernity with the echoes of ages past, producing an immersive and unique cultural experience.

Nightlife options in major cities

Transportation As the sun sets below the horizon, Turkey's major cities come alive with a dynamic nightlife that caters to a wide range of preferences, assuring memorable evenings for both locals and visitors. Istanbul, a city of contrasts, comes alive after dark. From sophisticated rooftop bars overlooking the Bosphorus to vibrant clubs on Istiklal Avenue, Istanbul's nightlife is as diverse as the city itself. Whether you like the rhythms foreign

DJs or the atmosphere of a traditional methane, the options are limitless.
Ankara, the capital, reveals its own midnight appeal. Kocatepe and Tunali Hilmi streets change into vibrant centers, with a variety of pubs and clubs to satisfy all tastes. The city's international environment assures a vibrant nightlife scene.
Cities along the coast, such as Izmir and Antalya, give the nighttime air a distinct coastal atmosphere. Seaside pubs, beach clubs, and waterfront lounges provide a great backdrop for those looking for a more relaxing yet lively evening.
Turkey's nightlife in 2024 welcomes exploration, promising a varied mix of modern entertainment and traditional flavors, making every night a celebration in this lively and diverse country.

CHAPTER NINE

Places to visit around the country

Turkey, a treasure mine of historical monuments and magnificent scenery, encourages travel beyond its teeming cities. In 2024, the Turkey Travel Guide will provide a plethora of intriguing spots to explore around the country.

Cappadocia: Marvel at the strange landscapes of Cappadocia, where fairy chimneys and cave homes provide an ethereal picture. Take a hot air balloon flight at dawn for an exquisite view.

Pamukkale: Discover Pamukkale's picturesque terraces, which are ornamented with mineral-rich hot springs. The sparkling white travertines and ancient Hierapolis provide a fascinating backdrop. Ascend Mount Nemrut to see massive stone monuments dating back to the Kingdom of Commagene. The dawn and sunset views from this UNESCO World Heritage site are breathtaking.

Antalya's Old Town: Discover the ancient beauty of Antalya's Old Town (Kaleiçi), with tiny lanes that reveal Ottoman-era buildings, busy bazaars, and the magnificent Hadrian's Gate.

Ephesus: Follow along the footsteps of ancient civilizations through the city's well-preserved remains, which include the Library of Celsus and the Great Theatre.

Pergamon: Climb the Acropolis of Pergamon to see ancient temples, a breathtaking amphitheater, and the Asclepius Sanctuary.

From the ancient wonders of Ephesus to the natural wonders of Cappadocia, Turkey's various landscapes and historical sites guarantee an interesting adventure for visitors in 2024.

Public transportation and car rentals

According to the Turkey Travel Guide 2024, navigating the country's different landscapes is facilitated by an efficient public transit system and easily available automobile rentals. For budget-conscious visitors looking for economical solutions, public transportation is a dependable option. In large cities including Istanbul, Ankara, and Izmir, extensive metro and bus networks provide inexpensive options to see metropolitan sites and beyond. Trains and intercity buses link many locations, making long-distance travel cost-effective.

Car rentals are easily accessible across Turkey for people who want the independence of their own automobile. To get the best deals, book in advance through trustworthy internet platforms or directly with local agents. Car rental services are available at major airports, city centers, and prominent tourist destinations,making it convenient for tourists arriving by plane or looking for a vehicle to explore.

In 2024, whether traversing Istanbul's crowded streets or taking a picturesque road trip through Cappadocia, the Turkey Travel Guide guarantees that passengers have easy access to both inexpensive public transit and low-cost vehicle rental alternatives for a pleasant and cost-effective experience.

CHAPTER TEN

Safety and Practical Tips

Having a safe and happy travel experience in Turkey requires a mix of knowledge, preparation, and cultural sensitivity. Here are safety and practical suggestions for tourists to Turkey in 2024.

Documentation and Healthcare:

Keep copies of your passport, visa, and other crucial documents. Store them separately from the originals.

Familiarize yourself with local emergency numbers and the nearest embassy or consulate.

Make sure you have adequate travel insurance that covers medical emergencies.

Cultural Respect:Respect local norms and dress modestly, especially in sacred areas.

Learn a few basic Turkish phrases; people appreciate visitors who attempt to communicate in their language.

Transport Safety: Use trustworthy transportation providers and be aware of unmarked cabs.

Follow the safety requirements for public transportation and keep your possessions secure.

Food and Water Safety: Enjoy the local cuisine, but be cautious with street food. Choose vendors who follow appropriate hygiene procedures.

To avoid waterborne infections, drink only bottled or filtered water.

Currency and finances:Inform your bank about your travel dates to avoid problems while using credit or debit cards.

Use ATMs with caution and avoid showing big quantities of cash.

Communication:For cost-effective communication, either get a local SIM card or activate your international roaming plan.

Stay in touch with your trip buddies and advise someone trustworthy about your daily plans.

Emergency Preparedness:Familiarize yourself with emergency exit routes in your lodging.

Keep emergency contact information ready, such as the phone numbers for local authorities and your country's embassy.

Local Advice: Seek information from locals or your hotel about safe and dangerous regions.

Stay informed about current events and any travel advisories issued by your government.

Weather Awareness:

Be cautious of local weather conditions, especially if you're visiting many places with different climates.

COVID-19 precautions:Stay up to date on the latest COVID-19 recommendations and follow all health and safety measures.
Carry essentials such as hand sanitizer and face masks.
In 2024, tourists may enjoy Turkey's beauty while emphasizing their safety and well-being by being educated, respecting local customs, and remaining cautious.

Travel advisories and safety considerations
the Turkey Travel Guide 2024, staying informed about travel advisories and prioritizing safety considerations is paramount for a secure and enjoyable journey. While Turkey is generally a safe destination, it's essential to be aware of any travel advisories issued by your home country and to stay updated on local conditions.
Check official government websites and consult with your country's embassy or consulate in Turkey for the latest information. Understand any specific safety concerns or areas that may require caution.

Register with your embassy upon arrival to receive important updates and assistance if needed.
While exploring Turkey's diverse regions, exercise standard safety precautions. Be mindful of your surroundings, avoid displaying valuable items, and use secure transportation options. Respect local customs and adhere to any regulations in place, especially concerning health and safety.
Stay connected with fellow travelers, inform someone trustworthy about your plans, and have emergency contact numbers readily available. Familiarize yourself with local emergency services and medical facilities.
In 2024, with a proactive approach to safety considerations and a keen awareness of travel advisories, visitors can relish the beauty of Turkey while ensuring a secure and memorable travel experience

Healthcare facilities and emergency service

According to the Turkey Travel Guide 2024, tourists may be certain that the nation has a well-established healthcare system and reliable emergency services. Major cities and famous tourist locations are equipped with modern hospitals, clinics, and medical facilities that provide high-quality care. Dial 112 for immediate medical help. English-speaking personnel are frequently accessible in metropolitan hospitals, allowing overseas visitors to communicate more effectively. It is recommended to get comprehensive travel insurance that covers medical bills to provide financial security in the event of an emergency.

Pharmacies, known as "eczane" in Turkish, are widely available, selling a variety of over-the-counter and prescription pharmaceuticals. Pharmacists are often competent and may help with minor medical issues.

In the event of a medical emergency, your country's embassy or consulate in Turkey can offer important support and advice. Familiarize yourself with the location of the nearest medical facilities and preserve a list of important contacts, such as local emergency numbers and your embassy's contact information.

Description of various hospitals in various locations

Travelers may explore Turkey with confidence in 2024, knowing that their well-being is emphasized thanks to a dependable healthcare system and readily available emergency services.
The following are descriptions of hospitals in various locations of Turkey for the Turkey Travel Guide 2024:

Istanbul: Acıbadem Maslak Hospital.
Acıbadem Maslak Hospital, situated in the middle of Istanbul, is a contemporary hospital institution with advanced technology. With an emphasis on patient-centered care, the hospital provides a diverse variety of medical services and specializations.

Ankara: Güven Hospital.
Güven Hospital in Ankara, located in the capital city, is well-known for providing excellent healthcare services. The hospital's staff of qualified specialists provides comprehensive medical care, including specialty treatments and operations.

Izmir: Ege University Medical Faculty Hospital.
The Ege University Medical Faculty Hospital in Izmir is a respected hospital affiliated with Ege University. The hospital, which is known for its academic brilliance and research activities, provides modern medical services as well as education.

Antalya: Medical Park. Antalya Hospital

Medical Park Antalya Hospital is a well-known healthcare center in the seaside city of Antalya. With an emphasis on patient comfort and well-being, the hospital offers a wide range of medical services, including basic healthcare and specialty therapies.

Cappadocia Region: Nevşehir State Hospital.
In Cappadocia's distinctive settings, Nevşehir State Hospital acts as a healthcare hub for both residents and tourists. The hospital provides necessary medical services to both inhabitants and tourists, assuring their well-being.
These facilities represent Turkey's broad healthcare environment, ensuring that tourists have access to high-quality medical treatments in all locations
While I can give information on pharmacies in various places, supplying precise price lists may not be possible owing to the dynamic nature of pricing and changes across pharmacies. However, below are descriptions of pharmacies in different parts of Turkey for the Turkey Travel Guide 2024:

Description of various pharmacy and there price list in various locations
Şahin Pharmacy in Taksim, Istanbul.

Şahin Pharmacy, located in Taksim, provides a variety of pharmaceuticals and over-the-counter goods. The team is skilled and can help with a variety of health concerns.

Ankara: Şafak Eczanesi (Şafak Pharmacy) at Kızılay.

Şafak Pharmacy, located in the center Kızılay neighborhood, offers convenient and courteous service. It meets the healthcare requirements of both residents and tourists to Ankara.

Izmir: Yaman Eczanesi (Yaman Pharmacy) - Alsancak

Yaman Pharmacy, located in Izmir's bustling Alsancak area, is a dependable source of pharmaceuticals. The pharmacy sells a wide range of drugs and offers individualized help.

Antalya: Güneş Eczanesi (Güneş Pharmacy)-Kaleiçi

Güneş Pharmacy, located in Antalya's ancient Kaleiçi neighborhood, caters to the health needs of visitors visiting the city's lovely old streets. The pharmacy provides a variety of items and drugs.

Cappadocia Region: Ürgüp Eczanesi (Urgüp Pharmacy)

In the picturesque region of Cappadocia, Ürgüp Pharmacy is a local healthcare provider that provides vital pharmaceutical services. Travelers in the region may rely on this drugstore for medical care.
These pharmacies illustrate the variety of healthcare services provided in various locations of Turkey, making it convenient and accessible to both inhabitants and visitors. Prices may vary, therefore it is best to contact directly with pharmacies directly for exact information.

Accommodation guide with price of different region

Istanbul:
Pera Palace Hotel, a historic hotel in Beyoğlu, offers luxurious rooms with renowned views. The prices range from $200 to $500 each night.
Mid-Range Option: The House Hotel Galatasaray: A boutique hotel in Galatasaray with chic décor. Prices range between $100 and $200 each night.
Cheers Lighthouse Hostel is a budget-friendly hostel near Sultanahmet. Dormitory costs start at $20 per night.
Cappadocia:Luxury Option - Museum Hotel: A cave hotel in Uçhisar with breathtaking views. Prices range between $300 and $700 per night.
Sultan Cave Suites, a mid-range option located in Göreme, offers unique cave rooms. Prices range between $150 and $300 per night.
Traveller's Cave Hotel: Budget-friendly accommodation in Göreme with lovely cave rooms. Prices start at $50 per night.
Antalya:
Luxury Option - Akra Hotel: A beachside hotel in Lara that provides exquisite amenities. The prices range from $200 to $500 each night.
*Mid-Range Option—MedDescriptions of lodging in various districts of Turkey for the Turkey Travel Guide 2024:

Hotel guide with price list, location and recommendation

Istanbul: Sultan's Haven Hotel, Sultanahmet
Sultan's Haven Hotel, located in the historic Sultanahmet area, combines modern luxury with classic charm. With views of prominent monuments such as the Hagia Sophia, this boutique hotel offers a one-of-a-kind and convenient stay in the center of Istanbul.
Ankara: Divan Cukurhan, Çankaya.
Divan Cukurhan is a beautiful hotel in Ankara's Çankaya neighborhood, housed in a painstakingly renovated caravanserai. Its central position makes it an excellent choice for business and leisure tourists seeking elegance and comfort.
Izmir: Key Hotel, Alsancak
Key Hotel in Izmir is located in the vibrant Alsancak area and provides a contemporary stay with an emphasis on modern design and services. Its closeness to major sights and active nightlife make it an ideal destination for travelers.

Antalya: Akra Hotel, Lara Akra Hotel, located in Antalya's Lara neighborhood, is a five-star hotel with breathtaking views of the Mediterranean. With contemporary amenities, several dining options, and a beachfront position, it offers a delightful stay on the Turkish Riviera.
Cappadocia Region: Cave Suites Hotel, Göreme Cave Suites Hotel in Göreme provides a one-of-a-kind experience amid Cappadocia's stunning surroundings, with cave-style rooms and modern conveniences. Nestled among fairyT chimneys, it offers a beautiful and evocative stay.

These lodgings highlight the variety of alternatives accessible across Turkey, from ancient neighborhoods in Istanbul to seaside luxury in Antalya and the unique cave homes of Cappadocia. For particular prices and availability, it is best to check with the hotels or booking sites closer to your vacation dates.

Description of resort guide with price list location and rccommendation

Descriptions of resorts in various regions of Turkey for the Turkey Travel Guide 2024 may not include particular costs due to the dynamic nature of pricing and variances across resorts. Below are descriptions of resorts in different regions:

Istanbul: Ajwa Hotel, Sultanahmet
Nestled in the heart of ancient Sultanahmet, Ajwa Hotel Sultanahmet is a luxury resort with Ottoman-inspired grandeur. With big accommodations, great cuisine, and a spa, it offers a luxurious escape in Istanbul.

Antalya: The Maxx Royal Belek Golf Resort
Maxx Royal Belek Golf Resort, located in Belek, is a beachside resort on the Turkish Riviera. This all-inclusive resort has a golf course, a private beach, and a variety of dining options, ensuring a sumptuous getaway.

Mandarin Oriental, Bodrum.
Mandarin Oriental, Bodrum is an elite resort located in the hills of the Bodrum Peninsula and overlooks the Aegean Sea. With private villas, a spa, and

gourmet restaurants, it provides a tranquil and refined hideaway.

Argos is located in the Cappadocia region.
In the breathtaking settings of Cappadocia, Argos in Cappadocia is a one-of-a-kind resort constructed within ancient caverns. With panoramic views and luxury facilities, it offers a unique and romantic experience.

Pamukkale: Doga Thermal Health & Spa.
Doga Thermal Health & Spa, located near Pamukkale's famed terraces, provides a wellness-focused resort experience. Thermal pools, spa services, and peaceful settings make this a perfect vacation in this natural beauty.

These resorts represent the range of luxury lodgings in Turkey. For detailed pricing and availability, we recommend contacting the resorts or booking platforms closer to your vacation dates.

Description of itinerary guide with price list location and recommendation

Here are some itineraries with projected pricing, locations, and recommendations for various regions of Turkey for the Turkey Travel Guide 2024:
Istanbul Extravaganza Duration: 4 days.
Prices range from moderate to high.
Day One: Sultanahmet Marvels
Visit Hagia Sophia and the Blue Mosque.
Explore Topkapi Palace's amazing exhibitions.
Day Two: Bosphorus Exploration
Take a sail around the Bosphorus for magnificent views.
Visit Dolmabahçe Palace and wander down Istiklal Avenue.
Day Three: Cultural Immersion
Discover the Grand Bazaar for unique shopping experiences.
Visit the Chora Church to see its magnificent mosaics.
Day Four: Modern Istanbul
Explore Taksim Square and the Beyoğlu area.
Istanbul Modern offers an opportunity to experience modern art.

Cappadocia Wonders
Duration: 3 days.
Price range: moderate.

Day one: Fairy Chimneys and Goreme.
Explore the Goreme Open Air Museum.
Take a hot-air balloon flight at dawn.
Day Two: Underground Cities
Visit Kaymakli and Derinkuyu Underground City.
Discover the beautiful rock formations of Love Valley.
Day three: Pasabag and Uchisar.
Explore Pasabag Valley's fairy chimneys.
Climb to the pinnacle of Uchisar Castle to see panoramic views.
Coastal Delights in Antalya
Duration: 5 days.
Prices range from moderate to high.
Day One: Old Town Antalya
Walk around Kaleiçi's old streets.
Visit Hadrian's Gate and the Hıdırlık Tower.
Day 2 - Perge and Aspendos
Explore the ancient remains of Perge.
Experience a performance at the Aspendos Theater.
Day three: Relax at Konyaalti Beach.
Enjoy a relaxing day at Konyaalti Beach.
Explore the Antalya Aquarium.
Day 4 - Duden Waterfalls
Visit the Lower Duden Waterfalls.

Take a boat cruise to view the Upper Duden Waterfalls.

Day 5: Trip to Olympus

Explore the ancient remains of Olympus.

Relax at Olympus Beach. These itineraries offer a glimpse into the many experiences that await visitors in various regions of Turkey. Prices may vary depending on hotel options and travel dates. For the exact price, check with appropriate travel companies or platforms closer to your chosen travel date.

CHAPTER ELEVEN

conclusion

Turkey Travel Guide 2024 promises an exciting voyage through a nation that perfectly mixes historical grandeur, natural beauty, and dynamic cultural encounters. Turkey's attractions are numerous, ranging from the renowned metropolis of Istanbul to the unearthly landscapes of Cappadocia and the clean beaches of Antalya. Travelers may enjoy excellent Turkish food, discover historic sites, and experience Turkish friendliness. Navigating the transit network, learning local traditions, and taking safety precautions create a seamless and enjoyable experience. With a plethora of lodgings, restaurants, and activities to suit all tastes and budgets, Turkey invites visitors to explore its timeless appeal in 2024. Whether seeking historical marvels, scenic wonders, or gastronomic pleasures, Turkey guarantees a riveting experience that will leave a lasting impression on those who visit its intriguing landscapes.

Made in the USA
Las Vegas, NV
21 February 2024

86033132R00056